the science of CATASTROPHE

MOVING EARTH

STEVE PARKER & DAVID WEST

Crabtree Publishing Company

www.crabtreebooks.com

Crabtree Publishing Company
www.crabtreebooks.com

Created and produced by:
  David West Children's Books
Project development and concept:
  David West Children's Books
Authors: Steve Parker and David West
Editor: Adrianna Morganelli
Proofreader: Crystal Sikkens
Designer: David West
Illustrator: David West
Project coordinator: Kathy Middleton
Production and print coordinator: Katherine Berti
Prepress technician: Katherine Berti

Library and Archives Canada Cataloguing in Publication

Parker, Steve, 1952-
  Natural disasters : moving earth / Steve Parker and David West.

(The science of catastrophe)
Includes index.
Issued also in electronic formats.
ISBN 978-0-7787-7576-8 (bound).--ISBN 978-0-7787-7581-2 (pbk.)

  1. Natural disasters--Juvenile literature. 2. Earth movements--Juvenile
literature. I. West, David, 1956- II. Title. III. Series: Science of catastrophe

GB5019.P375 2011   j904'.5   C2011-905019-6

Library of Congress Cataloging-in-Publication Data

Parker, Steve, 1952-
  Natural disasters. Moving Earth / Steve Parker & David West.
    p. cm. -- (The science of catastrophe)
  Includes index.
  ISBN 978-0-7787-7576-8 (reinforced library binding : alk. paper) -- ISBN 978-
0-7787-7581-2 (pbk. : alk. paper) -- ISBN 978-1-4271-8859-5 (electronic pdf) --
ISBN 978-1-4271-9762-7 (electronic html.)
  1. Natural disasters--Juvenile literature. 2. Earth movements--Juvenile
literature. I. West, David, 1956- II. Title. III. Title: Moving Earth. IV. Series.

  GB5019.P375 2012
  904'.5--dc23

                    2011027741

Crabtree Publishing Company

Printed in the U.S.A./112011/JA20111018

www.crabtreebooks.com   1-800-387-7650

Published in Canada
Crabtree Publishing
616 Welland Ave.
St. Catharines, Ontario
L2M 5V6

Published in the United States
Crabtree Publishing
PMB 59051
350 Fifth Avenue, 59th Floor
New York, New York 10118

Published in the United Kingdom
Crabtree Publishing
Maritime House
Basin Road North, Hove
BN41 1WR

Published in Australia
Crabtree Publishing
3 Charles Street
Coburg North
VIC 3058

Contents

In the township of Las Colinas, a massive section of the upper hillside slumps down onto hundreds of houses. (Artist's depiction)

Landslide

At 11:33 a.m. on January 13, 2001, an undersea earthquake near El Salvador's south coast set off landslides, mudslumps, and rockfalls across the country. Worst hit was Las Colinas, where more than 580 people died.

Las Colinas is a township of Santa Tecla, a large city near El Salvador's capital of San Salvador. The earthquake was felt strongly here, triggering more than 400 landslides in total. Most devastating was the slide that buried part of Las Colinas. It seems that the curved shape of the steep El Balsamo Ridge, south of the town, increased or amplified the size of the earth tremors. Gaps called tension cracks had already appeared along the ridge, but no one noticed these warning signs. The tremors loosened huge lumps of soil, mud, and small rocks high on the slope. As if scooped by a giant spoon, the lumps slid away to leave a bowl-shaped scar 330 feet (100 meters) across and 100 feet (30 meters) deep.

The mass of soil, more than a quarter of a million cubic yards (200,000 cubic meters), flowed like molasses down the lower slopes, and over houses and other buildings for 1,500 feet (457 meters). The whole slide took less than a minute to bury its victims.

THE SCIENCE OF LANDSLIDES

Deep soil remains on steep slopes, provided it does not get too wet, and tree roots help to keep it in position. But vibrations from an earthquake shake **bedrock** in the center of the ridge, loosen the soil, and set it in motion. Once it starts, it can surge like a thick liquid under its own immense crushing weight, across even the slightest slope.

1. Tension cracks appear as some areas of soil begin to slip slightly.

2. Sliding soil picks up trees, rocks, and debris.

bowl-shaped scar

Cliff Collapse

Tomas, the last hurricane of 2010, swept westward across the southern Caribbean. It left behind floods, wind damage, power outages, even a crashed airliner. One of the most sudden, catastrophic events was a huge cliff collapse at the high-class resort of Soufrière, on St. Lucia's west coast.

St. Lucia, one of the Windward Islands, is a well-known holiday paradise. But trouble in paradise comes every few years, in the shape of Atlantic hurricanes. Tomas was the 12th of the 2010 season, striking at the end of October. Although not the most powerful, it passed very close to St. Lucia.

Soufrière and neighboring Fond St. Jacques suffered the usual flooding, roofs blown away, and boats smashed on the waterfront. The storm, however, triggered another disaster—a cliff collapse. Fierce winds whipped up crashing waves that battered the tall cliffs near the beach. Already weak from years of gradual **erosion**, the rocks were **undercut** so much, they could no longer hold. They broke apart and fell like a stack of bricks, taking down dozens of dwellings from the clifftop community. More than 5,000 were made homeless. Across all of St. Lucia more than 70 people died. The cost of repairing Tomas's destruction was almost $700 million.

THE SCIENCE OF CLIFF COLLAPSE

Where huge waves pound the shore day after day, year after year, they wear away, or **erode**, even the hardest rock. At the base of a tall cliff the surging waters—often carrying pebbles or shingle from a previous cliff fall—gradually eat into, or undercut, the rock face. Eventually the weight of the cliff above is too much. It suddenly cracks and crashes down.

1. Erosion is greatest at the sea's surface level, where waves caused by strong winds batter into the rock every few seconds. Each local storm increases the wearing process.

2. The rate of wear depends on the type of rock—for example, granite is much harder and more resistant than chalk. But over years or centuries, the undercut increases.

undercut with wave platform beneath

3. The rock has so little support from below, its weight makes it split and fall in a catastrophic cliff collapse. The debris, picked up by waves, begins to undercut again.

rocks and debris smashed by waves

The devastating avalanche on Mont Blanc du Tacul picks up snow and speed. (Artist's depiction)

Avalanche

MONT BLANC DU TACUL, FRANCE, 2008

The European Alps had a bad year in 2008. More than 100 people died in a series of avalanches, icefalls, and rockslides on the high slopes. The avalanche of August 24 was one of the worst, claiming eight lives.

An avalanche is a sliding, falling mass of snow, often mixing with ice and rocks. As it tumbles down a steep slope, it can pick up stones, trees—and people, as at Mont Blanc du Tacul. This is one of the tallest Alpine peaks, at 13,937 feet (4,248 meters), only slightly lower than nearby Mont Blanc itself, Western Europe's highest mountain. On the fateful day, 47 climbers set off very early to reach the summit. The avalanche struck at 3 a.m., probably set off by a giant falling lump of ice called a **serac** loosened by summer warmth. As it slid, the serac dislodged a great slab of snow and ice to

THE SCIENCE OF AVALANCHES

There are several types of avalanches, but all need some kind of trigger to get going. Before this, warmth may melt the snow and ice, or they build up due to many falls and become so heavy that they start to crack under their own weight. Triggers include local earth tremors, hot Sun, or even a noise such as a gunshot, low-flying aircraft, snowmobile, or explosions from mines and quarries. The vibrations and roar from one avalanche often trigger more in the area.

fresh layer of snow

old snow layers turned to ice

1. Fresh, soft snow falls on earlier layers of snow that were melted by the daytime Sun and then frozen at night, creating slippery layers of ice.

cracks

2. The fresh snow needs only slight movement, warmth, or even a noise, to start slipping. Cracks may extend down to the deeper, more icy layers.

avalanche

3. Once the snow and ice start moving, friction with the stationary layer below melts their base to water. This acts to lubricate the slide, and the avalanche is under way.

form a rushing mass more than 160 feet (50 meters) wide. At 11,800 feet (3,596 meters) high, it hit the eight climbers and swept them more than 3,300 feet (1,000 meters) down the mountainside. Rescuers were in the area within an hour, but the bodies were only located a few days later by snow-penetrating radar. They were found under the ice block, 130 feet (40 meters) below the surface.

Mudslide

Vargas State, on Venezuela's north coast, looks out to the Caribbean Sea and is the nation's main transport hub. In mid-December 1999, one year's rain fell here in just three days, setting off huge mudslides and debris flows across the state.

The torrential December rains were unexpected since Venezuela's wet season usually fades during October. First, heavy storms on December 2–3 unleashed more than eight inches (20 centimeters) of rain, turning the soil into a sopping mess. Just two weeks later, from December 14, came a whole year's worth of rain, more than 36 inches (90 centimeters) in 55 hours. The amounts falling directly onto the area were joined by raging rivers flowing from high mountains to the south, through the state to the sea. The rivers were loaded with sand, soil, mud, and general debris swept down from the hill slopes. They burst their banks and overwhelmed channels specially made to route these floods away from built-up areas.

The channel system had been created because Vargas State had suffered mudslides before. Many of the communities were built on soft ground left behind by previous flows over hundreds and thousands of years. As the rivers carried their loads to the sea, they

THE SCIENCE OF MUDSLIDES

Soil, dirt, and earth become mud when plenty of water is added. Extra-heavy rains seep down or penetrate the soil to greater depth so that it becomes completely soaked, or saturated. The water works like a lubricant to allow soil particles to slip past each other. Gradually the slippery mass begins to slide

1. Heavy rainfall on hills flows down through, rather than over, the soil.

soil layer

underlying rock layer

slowed down on flatter land and dropped their sediments as large, spreading deltas called **alluvial fans**. December's rainfall had penetrated deep, turning the ground into a thick, oozing, semi-liquid that flowed even on the shallowest slopes. The mud slid at speeds of up to 50 feet (15 meters) per second. Los Corales neighborhood was one of the hardest hit, as mud up to 16 feet (5 meters) deep surged through. Picking up rocks and other debris, it swept away cars, trees, small dwellings, and people. Over the whole of Vargas State, up to 25,000 people died in the disaster and 80,000 were made homeless.

down almost any slope. As the mudslide increases speed and volume, it picks up rocks, trees, and other items, and becomes a debris flow. Where the ground flattens out, the flow slows and ceases. But the damage is immense. Unlike floodwater, which gradually seeps away, the stinking mud simply stays where it was dumped.

2. Saturated soil becomes liquid and slides down the hillside, gathering speed.

mudflow follows steepest route

Volcanic Eruption

During North America's biggest recorded volcanic eruption, in U.S.A.'s Washington State, Mount St. Helens blew its top off—or rather, blasted its side away. Part earthquake, part explosion, and part eruption, the massive event spread damage more than 50 miles (80 kilometers).

Mount St. Helens is in the far northwest of the U.S.A., 100 miles (160 kilometers) south of Seattle. It had long been a scenic attraction, famous for its steam plumes and puffs of ash clouds. During March and April 1980, scientists noticed an increase in earth tremors and advised the authorities to close the area to the public. Then on May 18, 1980, the mountain let rip. A mass of underground molten (melted) rock, **magma**, had pushed up beneath the volcano, pressing especially under its north side. The gigantic force bulged and split the rocks and blew off the north flank, which rained rockfalls as it slid down.

THE SCIENCE OF VOLCANIC ERUPTIONS

Red-hot, runny rock called magma rises under immense pressure from deep inside Earth, up through weak spots to explode out as a volcanic eruption. Volcanic bombs—glowing hot rocks as big as trucks—fly through the air. Choking gases and ash are thrown to enormous height, disrupting air travel. Red-hot rock runs slowly like a river down the slope as **lava** flows. Much faster are lahars, which are speedy combinations of ash, dust, gases, and boulders all mixed with water, as described on later pages.

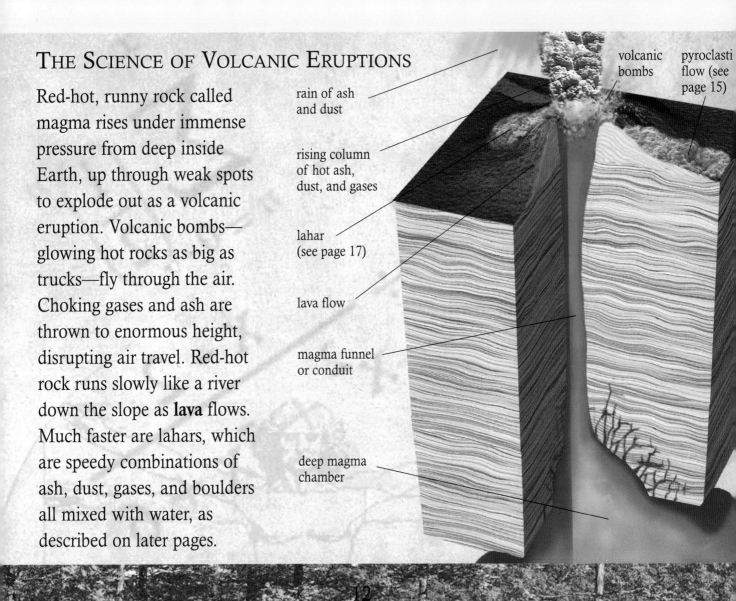

rain of ash and dust

rising column of hot ash, dust, and gases

volcanic bombs

pyroclastic flow (see page 15)

lahar (see page 17)

lava flow

magma funnel or conduit

deep magma chamber

This released the pressure and the magma spurted up to the surface, becoming lava. It burst out as a mix of red-hot rocks, boulders, mud, ash, and gases. Glaciers (frozen rivers) high on the peak melted in the heat and mixed in. The whole mass surged down the slopes at incredible speed as a series of pyroclastic flows (see page 15). Some spread as far as 40 miles (65 kilometers), scorching and blasting trees and buildings into pieces. Ash clouds rose 75,000 feet (23,000 meters) high and fell on 11 neighboring states.

The destruction was on an epic scale. The mountain ended up 1,313 feet (400 meters) lower, at 8,365 feet (2,550 meters), with a vast scoop out of its north side. Because people were warned to stay away, the death toll was astonishingly low—57.

Mount St. Helens gets ready to blow its top and blast away most of one side of its peak. (Artist's depiction)

THE SCIENCE OF BLASTS AND FLOWS

Not all volcanoes erupt neatly from a small crater at the top of a dome- or cone-shaped mountain. There are many kinds of eruptions depending on the contents, pressure, and direction of the magma, and the strength of the overlying rock layers. In June 1991, the eruption of Mount Pinatubo, in the Philippines, sent up so much ash that it fell to choke land and rivers far around, and darkened the skies around the whole world as it spread in high-level winds. Like boiling milk, Mount Lamington in Papua New Guinea continued to send out pyroclastic flows after its biggest eruption in 1951. On the Caribbean island of Martinique in 1902, Mount Pelée had several eruptions. One massive pyroclastic flow, when part of the dome fell in, killed 30,000 people in nearby St. Pierre.

ashes and gases

vertical eruption and column collapse (Mount Pinatubo, Soufrière Hills)

pyroclastic and lava flows

sideways blast blows away part of volcano (Mount St. Helens, see page 12)

low pressure "boiling over" (Mount Lamington)

dome collapse (Mount Pelée)

The main pyroclastic flow races down the Soufrière hillside at immense speed during the great eruption of 1997. (Artist's depiction)

Pyroclastic Flow

SOUFRIÈRE HILLS VOLCANOES, MONTSERRAT, 1997

Red-hot rivers of runny lava and flying blocks of rock hurled out by a volcano are scary enough. But "racing cloud of death" and *nuée ardente* (glowing cloud) are among the names for the most feared part of many eruptions—the pyroclastic flow. This is often the real mass killer.

"Pyroclastic" means fiery broken-apart pieces. The pyroclastic flow is a mix of superhot gases, ash, small rock particles, steam, and other material thrown out by the volcano, as if by a giant belch or burp. The flow can be up to 1,500 degrees Fahrenheit (816 degrees Celsius), so hot that it glows in daylight. It sweeps downhill like a high-speed avalanche at more than 500 miles per hour (805 kilometers per hour). Everything in its path is burned to pieces until it loses speed and heat, and fades away. This could be more than 100 miles (161 kilometers) from its source volcano.

One of the worst pyroclastic flows in recent times was on the Caribbean island of Montserrat. Soufrière Hills is a set of several volcanoes that had been **dormant** or resting for more than a hundred years. But small eruptions began in 1995. Then on June 25, 1997 a major "blow" sent several pyroclastic flows blasting across the island. The scorching clouds destroyed the island's airport, killed 19 people, and almost wiped out the tourist industry. Eruptive flows have continued on and off since, making more than half of the island unsuitable for people.

THE SCIENCE OF LAHARS

Volcanoes throw out all kinds of materials—but these are too hot to contain liquid water. However, if water is then added to the recipe, perhaps from heavy rain, melting snow, ice fields, or glaciers high on the mountain, the result is a fast-moving tide of dust, particles, rock fragments, and general debris. It swishes along like ready-mixed cement or concrete, reaching speeds of up to 60 miles per hour (97 kilometers per hour).

The deadly lahar swamps a village near Armero. (Artist's depiction)

1. A volcano erupts with hot ash, rock fragments, dust, gases, and lava.

2. Hot ash falling on the slopes melts snow, ice, and glaciers.

3. Lava flows also melt glaciers, ice, and snow.

4. Pyroclastic flows add to the melting of ice, snow, and glaciers.

5. Lahars form from meltwater and ejected volcanic material.

6. Lahars pick up clay, mud, soil, rocks, and debris as they pour across the landscape.

Lahar

ARMERO, COLOMBIA, 1985

Lahars are particular kinds of volcanic outpourings mixed with plenty of water, like tides of freshly-mixed concrete. The town of Armero, in west-central Colombia, was virtually destroyed by one, with more than 20,000 deaths.

Colombia is no stranger to earthquakes, volcanic eruptions, severe floods, and other natural disasters. In September 1985, scientists detected earth movements from Nevado del Ruiz, a volcano that had been inactive for almost 70 years. They strongly warned the government to advise people to leave the area. Unfortunately, the government didn't listen. Then on November 13, without warning at about 9 p.m., a major eruption shook the region. The volcano's rock fragments, dust, ash, and lava melted glaciers high on the cold slopes, and mixed into four huge lahars that poured down the mountainside, along gullies and channels where usually glacier meltwater trickled. Moving at 40 miles per hour (65 kilometers per hour), the lahars picked up clay and soil from the land and surged onward. The nearby town of Armero was engulfed in minutes, and two-thirds of the people died. Losses in other villages and towns brought the number of deaths to 23,000. Shaken by the great tragedy, the Colombian people blamed, not the volcano, but the government for not ordering an evacuation.

Lake Overturn

Few natural catastrophes are as silent as the lake eruption or lake overturn. It is like shaking a giant soda-pop bottle and letting it fizz and bubble to release deadly gases—as happened in Africa in 1986.

Very special conditions are needed to produce a lake overturn, sometimes known as an "exploding lake." Only three sites are known so far, all in West Africa—Lakes Nyos and Monoun, both in Cameroon, and Lake Kivu in the Democratic Republic of Congo. What actually happened at Lake Nyos on August 24, 1986, is not clear since there are no eyewitnesses. The scientific evidence shows that for centuries, the gas carbon dioxide, CO_2, had been collecting deep in this lake, which is in a bowl-shaped crater high on the side of an inactive volcano. The CO_2 was dissolved in the water, rather than as gas bubbles, and concentrated in the cold, highly pressurized layer near the lake bed. Much of the CO_2 came from magma below, inside the volcano. Some kind of trigger, perhaps a landslide within the lake itself, disturbed this settled situation. The CO_2-rich waters swirled to the surface. As the pressure reduced, the gas came out of the solution, just like opening a fizzy carbonated-drink container (the "fizz" in that being the same gas, CO_2). The CO_2

frothed out in a bubbling fountain up to 300 feet (91 meters) high. Once released, the CO_2 gas—which is heavier or denser than air—flowed away down the mountainside. It was a silent, invisible, deadly cloud, because CO_2 is poisonous to the body and causes lack of oxygen, breathing problems, and suffocation. The cloud moved at up to 30 miles per hour (50 kilometers per hour) across fields, villages, and farms, and remained concentrated enough to kill for up to 15 miles (25 kilometers). More than 1,700 people and other living things, from cattle to birds, perished in the villages of Nyos, Cha, Kam, and Subum.

Thousands of cattle silently suffocate as gases spread from Lake Nyos. (Artist's depiction)

THE SCIENCE OF LAKE OVERTURNS

An overturn, also known as an outgassing, happens when a sudden event disturbs the quiet conditions in a particular kind of lake. The lake must have magma nearby, usually several miles (kilometers) below. The magma gives off CO_2 which seeps upward and concentrates near the lake bed, where the water is cold and under great pressure. Lake Nyos is ideal, being 680 feet (207 meters) deep.

1. Water seeps down into a volcanic plug.

deep lake in bowl of volcano

2. CO_2 from the magma is displaced by the water and rises.

3. Dissolved CO_2 collects in the cold water in the lower part of the lake.

magma

4. An earth tremor or a landslide in the lake disturbs the CO_2, which bubbles to the surface.

6. Heavy CO_2 hugs the ground as it flows downward.

5. CO_2 escapes from the lake's surface and spreads.

Deadly debris rains down in the streets of Haiti. (Artist's depiction)

THE SCIENCE OF FAULT-SLIP EARTHQUAKES

crust

mantle

convection currents in mantle

tectonic plates of crust are moved by mantle currents beneath

outer core

inner core

Around the center or core of Earth is the mantle, a layer of hot, semi-liquid, slowly-moving rock. Gigantic swirling currents here affect the thin outermost layer of solid rock, the crust. This is cracked like a broken eggshell into many enormous, curved, jagged-edged pieces called tectonic plates. As the mantle moves, the currents push the plates, which sometimes stick together—and then slip.

Fault-Slip Earthquake

At 4:53 p.m. local time on January 12, 2010, the Caribbean island of Haiti shook to a huge earthquake. In the following chaos and mayhem, up to 100,000 people died. As the full scale of the catastrophe became clear, two million people found themselves homeless.

EARTHQUAKE SEQUENCE

friction

1. Tectonic plates try to move past each other at their edges or faults, but often they lock due to friction. Over time, vast stresses and tensions build up.

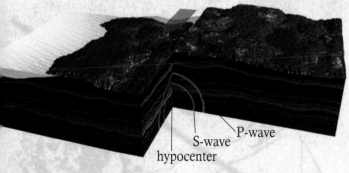

S-wave P-wave
hypocenter

2. The stresses get so great that the plates suddenly slip, releasing stored energy as an earthquake. The main energy release is at the hypocenter. Sideways, squeeze-stretch P-waves spread first, then up-and-down, ripple-like S-waves.

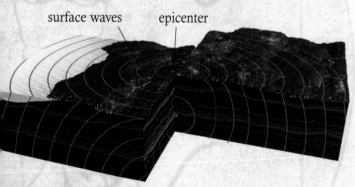

surface waves   epicenter

3. The third set of waves are surface waves, which spread through Earth's surface rocks from the epicenter—the place directly above the hypocenter. These can be so powerful that they go all around the world.

The Haiti earthquake measured 7.0 on the Moment Magnitude Scale. It resulted from a slip between two of the great curved sections of Earth's outer crust, called **tectonic plates**—the Caribbean and North American plates. It was especially destructive because the central point of the slippage, called the **hypocenter**, was shallow for an earthquake, only eight miles (13 kilometers) deep. The ground rocked by several feet but there was no huge gash or split at the surface, as with many earthquakes.

The huge tremors were felt most directly at the **epicenter**, some 15 miles (25 kilometers) west of the island's capital, Port-au-Prince. Their energy was so great that they devastated much of the island. Haiti is a poor nation with little money to spend on strong, earthquake-resistant buildings, roads, electricity networks, water distribution, and other **infrastructure**. Vast areas of buildings, from modern office blocks to shanty shacks, were reduced to rubble. Roads were blocked and sewage systems split open, bringing the risk of diseases such as cholera. Rich nations rushed to help, but it will be 10 years or more before the island can recover.

Subduction Quake-Tsunami

A subduction zone is where one of Earth's enormous tectonic plates slides underneath another. On March 11, 2011, the Tohoku region of Japan experienced a "megathrust" subduction earthquake and a colossal **tsunami** wave (described on the page 24).

The Tohoku region is on the northeast of Japan's main island, Honshu. The earthquake was centered 44 miles (70 kilometers) east of its coast, and 20 miles (32 kilometers) deep— quite shallow for an earthquake. It registered 9.0 on the Moment Magnitude Scale, putting it in the Top Five Quakes ever recorded. The power was so massive that it made the north of Honshu more than seven feet (two meters) wider, shifted parts of it up to 16 feet (five meters) closer to North America, and lowered the east coast in places by more than five feet (1.5 meters). Many newer buildings in Japan are designed to resist earth tremors and most withstood the vibrations. But smaller, older structures, especially in the suburbs and villages, were shaken to the ground. Along with the following tsunami (see page 24), vast areas were destroyed. The death toll of 23,000 could only be estimated because many bodies were swept out to sea, or buried too deeply in mud and rubble to be recovered.

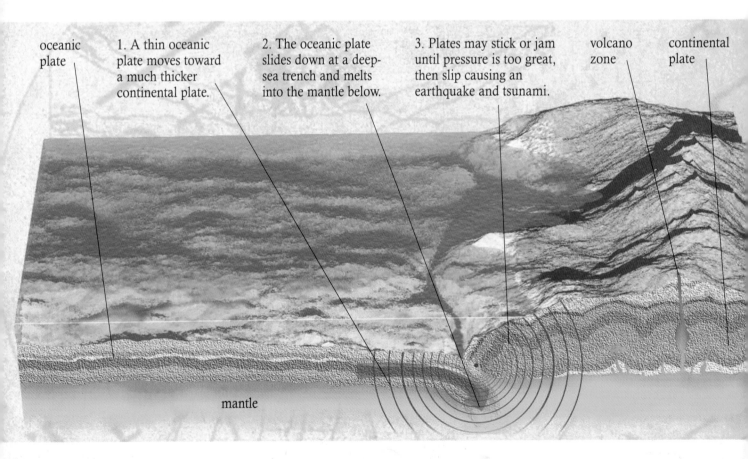

oceanic plate

1. A thin oceanic plate moves toward a much thicker continental plate.

2. The oceanic plate slides down at a deep-sea trench and melts into the mantle below.

3. Plates may stick or jam until pressure is too great, then slip causing an earthquake and tsunami.

volcano zone

continental plate

mantle

Older buildings in Sendai, the largest city near the Tohoku catastrophe, could not withstand violent shaking. (Artist's depiction)

THE SCIENCE OF SUBDUCTION EARTHQUAKES

There are two main kinds of tectonic plates, oceanic and continental. **Oceanic plates** are usually less then seven miles (10 kilometers) thick, while **continental plates**, carrying the major land masses, can be six times thicker. As deep mantle currents slide an oceanic plate toward a continental one, the oceanic plate is pushed or subducted below its thicker, heavier neighbor. The plates often lock or jam for years due to friction, until the pressure builds to make them jerk past, as described for fault-slip earthquakes on page 21.

Tsunami

The subduction earthquake of March 11, described on pages 22–23, set off a deadly wave of destruction—real ocean waves called tsunamis. These swamped a huge length of Japan's northeast coast.

The cause of the undersea 'quake near the Tohoku region of Honshu, Japan's main island, is described on page 22. As the sea floor moved, in places by as much as 100 feet (30 meters), the gigantic forces had another effect—they created huge ripples and waves called tsunamis. To the north, east, and south, these gradually faded into the vast Pacific. But as they headed east, they soon encountered Honshu's shallow coastal waters, reared up, and flooded inland. At the closest place to the earthquake, the tsunamis came ashore within 15 minutes. Depending on the shape of the coast, in some places the tsunamis were funneled and channeled to heights greater than 100 feet (30 meters).

The tsunami surges ashore along the east coast of Honshu, Japan. (Artist's depiction)

Within one hour the airport at Sendai City had been swept away. In some places the waves pushed more than 6 miles (10 kilometers) inland. They flooded farms, destroyed towns and cities, swept away roads and bridges, and tossed around a railroad train like a toy. Electricity networks, communications, gas and water supplies were wiped out. At Fukushima, the earthquake and tsunami worked together to damage the nuclear power plant. As deadly radiation began to leak from it, people were evacuated for 12 miles (20 kilometers) around. The double catastrophe killed over 23,000 people and made 300,000 homeless.

THE SCIENCE OF TSUNAMIS

subduction or fault-slip earthquake

undersea mudslump, rockfall, or landslide

sea floor collapse

Put your hand deep in a bathtub of water, and push strongly. Ripples and waves quickly splash around the edge. A tsunami begins in a similar way, by a great earth movement giving an immense "push" to the water around. The underwater force may be an earthquake, a large slide of mud or rocks on the seabed, or perhaps where the ocean floor collapses into a widening gap between two tectonic plates.

The pressure sets the water in motion as a series of massive ripples spreading upward and outward through the ocean. Their speed is amazing—up to 500 miles per hour (800 kilometers per hour). Like regular waves, tsunamis slow down and grow in height as they reach shallow water.

A tsunami becomes taller in shallow water and breaks onto shore.

Caldera Collapse

YELLOWSTONE, UNITED STATES, 640,000 YEARS AGO

Calderas are giant bowl-, crater- or cauldron-shaped features caused by volcanic activity. The U.S.A.'s Yellowstone area, in the northwest of Wyoming and nearby, has a long history of caldera formation.

Calderas around Yellowstone can be traced back more than five million years. It seems that the North American tectonic plate slides slowly above a zone of particularly active, upthrusting magma, called a geological hotspot. Huge volcanoes or even "super-volcanoes" form here. Then, as the plate moves on past the hotspot, they collapse into calderas, while a new set of volcanoes is created behind them, above the hardly-moving hotspot. This has happened many times over the Yellowstone hotspot. The most recent main event was the formation of the Yellowstone Caldera some 640,000 years ago. In this tremendous upheaval, 1,000 times more volcanic material was blasted out than by Mount St. Helens (described on earlier pages). With the magma below mostly gone or shrunk away, the surface rocks fell down to create a massive crater-like depression 50 miles (80 kilometers) long and 30 miles (48 kilometers) wide, and as deep as 3,300 feet (1,005 meters).

Different creatures roamed then, such as the huge-tusked American mastodon, a cousin of mammoths and elephants, and giant or long-horned bison, which were distant ancestors of today's bison. An even larger eruption, over twice the size of Yellowstone Caldera's, made the nearby Island Park Caldera over two million years ago.

THE SCIENCE OF CALDERAS

Some volcanoes erupt most of their molten rock, or magma, so that the chamber beneath becomes empty. Or the magma may cool and shrink away as a result of tectonic plate movements and magma currents. Left without support from below, the rocks of the crust fall into the "hole." This can happen in one explosive event, or in stages over many hundreds or thousands of years. The result is the great crater-like cauldron, the caldera.

rocks crack and weaken

magma chamber

1. Magma pushes up against the crust, creating cracks in a "roof" of rock.

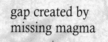

gap created by missing magma

2. Magma cools and shrinks, or erupts, leaving the roof unsupported.

rock roof collapses

3. The overlying rock falls inward, often in ring-shaped portions.

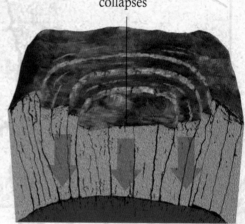

The colossal collapse of the Yellowstone Caldera was well before the last Ice Age. (Artist's depiction)

Asteroid Impact

During Earth's immense history, 4,600 million years, the planet has been hit by countless items flying through space. Every now and then is a "Big One"—a strike by an asteroid, comet, or large meteorite.

One of these major impacts probably happened around 65.5 million years ago. Scientists estimate it was an object about 6 miles (10 kilometers) across—probably a small asteroid, or a piece from a larger asteroid. It smashed into the planet at 12 miles per second (20 kilometers per second) and set off huge earthquakes, megatsunamis taller than today's skyscrapers, and volcanic explosions and eruptions that make modern ones look puny. The probable site for the impact is the Chicxulub Crater, a great depression half under the north coast of Mexico's Yucatan Peninsula, half undersea in the neighboring Gulf of Mexico. The crater, now partly obscured by seafloor mud and new land, is over 110 miles (175 kilometers) across. In the catastrophes that followed, whole groups of animals died out in what is known as the End-of-Cretaceous **mass extinction**.

1. impact site

2. shock or seismic waves

3. earthquakes, tsunamis, and volcanic eruptions

4. climate change with global cooling

5. shift in rotation axis

core

crust

mantle

THE SCIENCE OF IMPACTORS FROM SPACE

When a space rock hits Earth, it triggers a whole series of catastrophes. The actual impact causes seismic waves that make Earth vibrate like a bell. This disturbs tectonic plates which slip, generating earthquakes and tsunamis and setting off vast volcanic eruptions. Thrown-up ash and dust blot out the Sun, leading to cooling for years or even centuries. The jolt may even knock the planet into a different angle as it spins daily on its axis, leading to new worldwide climate patterns.

They included the dinosaurs (except for their descendants, the birds), flying pterosaurs, swimming plesiosaurs and mosasaurs, as well as shelled ammonites, and many kinds of plants. Evidence from fossils and rocks formed at this time support the impact theory. Why many creatures survived, including turtles, lizards, birds, and our own group, mammals, is still a puzzle.

A worried Tyrannosaurus rex *watches the fireball rock that will signal the end of the Age of Dinosaurs and the Cretaceous Period. (Artist's depiction)*

Disasters World Map

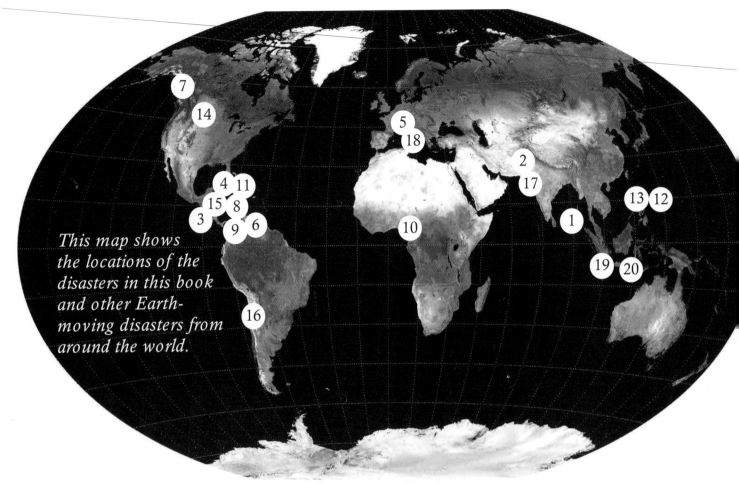

This map shows the locations of the disasters in this book and other Earth-moving disasters from around the world.

1. Indian Ocean Tsunami, 2004
2. Kohistan Avalanche, Pakistan, 2010
3. Las Colinas Landslide, El Salvador, 2001
4. Soufrière Cliff Collapse, St. Lucia, 2010
5. Mont Blanc du Tacul Avalanche, France, 2008
6. Vargas State Mudslide, Venezuela, 1999
7. Mount St. Helens Eruption, United States, 1980
8. Soufrière Hills Volcanoes Pyroclastic Flow, Montserrat, 1997
9. Armero Lahar, Colombia, 1985
10. Lake Nyos Overturn, Cameroon, 1986
11. Haiti Fault-Slip Earthquake, 2010
12. Subduction Megathrust Earthquake, Tohoku, Japan, 2011
13. Tsunami, Tohoku, Japan, 2011
14. Yellowstone Caldera Collapse, United States, 640,000 years ago
15. Asteroid Impact, Global Mass Extinction, 65.5 million years ago
16. Chile Earthquake, 2010
17. Gujarat Earthquake, India, 2001
18. Mount Vesuvius Eruption, Italy, AD 79
19. Krakatoa Eruption, Indonesia, 1883
20. Tambora Eruption, Indonesia, 1815

Glossary

alluvial fan A fan- or delta-shaped area of mud, sand, and other particles carried by a river that slows as it reaches a plain, so the particles can spread and settle

bedrock Solid rock under the plants, soil, stones, and loose rocks of an area

continental plate One of the thicker tectonic plates that carries a major land mass or continent, and may be more than 30 miles (50 kilometers) deep

dormant A volcano that has been inactive or "asleep," but which might become active and erupt again in the future

epicenter The place on the surface that is directly above the hypocenter or focus of an earthquake

erode, erosion Wear away rocks and other materials by wind, rain, ice, heat, cold, and other natural conditions

hypocenter The place where the main energy of an earthquake is released, usually deep below the surface, also called the focus of the earthquake

infrastructure All the structures, networks, and systems needed for smooth running of a region and daily life, such as roads, railways, ports, airports, bridges, tunnels, electricity and water and gas supplies, sewers, and communications

lava Very hot, molten or melted rocks at the surface. Before this, when it was below the surface, it was magma. Lava which has cooled and hardened may still be called lava.

magma Very hot, molten or melted rocks beneath the surface. When magma reaches the surface it is called lava.

mass extinction When many kinds of living things, including various plants and animals, all die out or become extinct at the same time

oceanic plate One of the thinner tectonic plates that lies underneath an ocean or sea, and which is usually less than seven miles (10 kilometers) deep

serac Large block, tower, or column of ice, formed where crevasses (cracks) join in a glacier, or where snow collects and freezes

tectonic plates Large, curved, rough-edged, slowly-moving pieces that together make up the rocky outer layer of Earth

tsunami A wall of moving water triggered by an earthquake

undercut Eroding or wearing away the lower part of a rocky area, such as a cliff, to leave an overhang above

Index